NO SKIN IN THE GAME

The God of the Jehovah's Witness

Frank H. Armstrong

NO SKIN IN THE GAME

Copyright © 2016 by Frank H. Armstrong

All rights reserved. No part of this book may be reproduced or transmitted in any form or by any means without written permission of the author.

ISBN-13: 978-0692772850
ISBN-10: 0692772855

Cover design by Brad Knefelkamp

THE HOLY BIBLE, NEW INTERNATIONAL VERSION®, NIV®
Copyright © 1973, 1978, 1984, 2011 by Biblica, Inc.® Used by permission. All rights reserved worldwide.

Scripture taken from the NEW AMERICAN STANDARD BIBLE®, Copyright © 1960, 1962, 1963, 1968, 1971, 1972, 1973, 1975, 1977, 1995 by The Lockman Foundation. Used by permission.

Scripture quotations marked HCSB are taken from the Holman Christian Standard Bible®, Copyright © 1999, 2000, 2002, 2003, 2009 by Holman Bible Publishers. Used by permission. Holman Christian Standard Bible®, Holman CSB®, and HCSB® are federally registered trademarks of Holman Bible Publishers.

The Holy Bible: International Standard Version. Release 2.0, Build 2015.02.09. Copyright © 1995-2014 by ISV Foundation. ALL RIGHTS RESERVED INTERNATIONALLY. Used by permission of Davidson Press, LLC.

Table of Contents

1. Metanarrative..1
2. Shared Glory..11
3. Mediating Messiah 23
4. The Divine Likeness of Jesus Christ 31
5. Appendix 43

Preface

This brief apologetic was borne of discussions I had with several Jehovah's Witnesses who graced my doorstep over the span of a few years, not many years ago, and of the subsequent conversations we enjoyed at a nearby Kingdom Hall.

I must confess that I am a rather hapless and unwitting evangelist (unlike my JW friends), preferring the scriptural mandate to "seek to live a quiet life" over that of "go therefore and make disciples." Nevertheless, I take to heart the admonition of the apostle Peter to be ready to give a reason for the hope I have within me—so here I am, and here are the results of those dialogues.

Through it all I learned that the popular literature which addresses JW doctrine doesn't adequately appraise the effect their view of Christ has on the biblical metanarrative. The usual approach is to amass a wealth of proof texts on various topics with which to convince the JW of his errors. Of course, the JW is notoriously well-equipped with a similar armament, thus turning a characteristic engagement into something of a scrum as one side argues past the other. Naturally, I discovered this shotgun approach to be insufficient, primarily because it fails to address the core issue which is the distinctive proxy status that Jehovah gives to Jesus Christ as the Son of Man and the Son of God *and what that means for the identity of God*.

Fundamentally, when the gospel of Jesus Christ is understood to be the good news of *someone else*, there are significant implications for our understanding of God. When scripture commends the perfect love of God with particular and repeated appeals to the person and work of Jesus Christ (*someone else* according to JWs), the biblical metanarrative fractures and the glory of God is diminished. Conversely, when we see the person of Jesus Christ in orthodox terms, the biblical metanarrative coheres and the glory of God abounds commensurate with that glorious paradox: God humbled himself (not *someone else*) to glorify us with Him.

I respectfully offer the following to the many Jehovah's Witnesses who minister door-to-door, and also to the individuals who will answer the door and minister from the other side.

Frank Armstrong

To Heather, Afton, and Kellen
The loves of my life

Introduction

A.W. Tozer wrote that what comes into our minds when we think about God is the most important thing about us because we tend to move toward our mental image of God.[1] Accordingly, if our thoughts about God are true and we are single-minded, then all is well with our souls. But if our thoughts about God are not true, then we find ourselves moving toward a false image of God, even if by degree. For example:

- A legalistic Christian betrays his belief in a loving God when, as a matter of course, he portrays an angry God to the world.
- Purveyors of a prosperity gospel often conflate the Good News and the American Dream (or its parallel) and portray a trifling, parochial God to the world.
- Those who deny the deity of Jesus Christ, such as the Jehovah's Witnesses, portray a strangely divested and principally unjust God to the world.

Admittedly, it is true that we only know in part, so our thoughts about God will be imperfect until that day in which we know fully just as we are fully known (1 Cor 13:12); nevertheless, it is possible to honor or dishonor God by the things we believe about Him.

If you agree that it is vitally important to think rightly about God, then the following words of Jesus Christ to his disciples have special relevance for you:

He asked His disciples, "Who do the people say that the Son of Man is?"

And they said, "Some say John the Baptist; others, Elijah; still others, Jeremiah or one of the prophets."

"But you," He asked them, "who do you say that I am?"

Simon Peter answered, "You are the Messiah, the Son of the living God!"

And Jesus responded, "Simon son of Jonah, you are blessed because flesh and blood did not reveal this to you, but my Father in heaven" (Mt. 16:13-17, HCSB).

What exactly did the Father reveal to Peter when he equated the Son of Man with the Son of God in the person of the Messiah? Who does scripture say Jesus is? These are the primary questions I am concerned with in the pages that follow, but before we address them we will consider the broader context—the big picture—provided by scripture.

1. Metanarrative

The Big Picture

When considering any topic it is possible to isolate individual details to the detriment of an accurate representation of the whole—to miss the forest for the trees, as it were. Seeing the big picture is important because it helps to ensure that the details are in proper relation to each other. The big picture, or the metanarrative, provides context for the details.

To illustrate the importance of metanarrative, imagine a person getting dressed who thinks he's fairly well put together only to find when he stands before a full-length mirror that the pieces don't go together at all. His plaid flannel shirt clashes with his argyle tie, pinstriped slacks, and rainbow socks. A view of the whole is essential to discerning whether the individual pieces fit together properly.

Better yet, think of a jigsaw puzzle. We all know how important the picture on top of the box is to completing a puzzle. In fact, doing a puzzle is the process of momentarily matching wrong pieces, realizing they don't fit, and then finding the right pieces which do fit, all with the aid of that big picture. Sometimes we force pieces together and immediately recognize the mistake, and sometimes we fit pieces together easily by virtue of their complementary shapes only to find that the picture spanning the pieces is misaligned, so we must re-evaluate. What we find in the process, remarkably, is that the big picture is the most important piece of the puzzle—it is the *whole piece*. The whole piece must fit, and this is why we must mind the metanarrative.

Metanarrative

Biblical Metanarrative: The Love of God

It is imperative that we mind the biblical metanarrative when considering the debate between orthodox Christianity and religious groups that deny the deity of Jesus Christ, such as the Jehovah's Witnesses (JW), because it will help us to correctly answer the question that Jesus asked of himself: "Who do you say that I am?"

Discussions with JWs often devolve into a volley of proof texts for individual doctrines. The terms *begotten* and *firstborn*, the meaning of words in the original Greek, and verb tenses are just the sort of minutiae that is parsed and examined in the course of debate. While these details are important, it is essential that we step back to ensure our understanding of them comports with the big picture provided by scripture. So, where do we begin? What is the metanarrative that scripture provides and how does it inform our understanding of the nature of Jesus Christ and of God? Fortunately, I think we can begin where there is practically universal agreement: the love of God.

The love of God is ubiquitous in the pages of scripture. From the creation of mankind in the book of Genesis to our re-creation in the book of Revelation, God's love is everywhere on display. The apostle John tells us that "God is love" (1 Jn 4:8), and we know intuitively that nobody loves us like God does. Indeed, for Christians the love of God is the singular animating fact of life; therefore, the metanarrative that scripture provides speaks first and foremost to God's love. With this in mind, I submit that John 3:16 is arguably the most recognized bible verse precisely because it summarizes the whole of scripture so well with particular reference to God's love, so let us begin there:

For God so loved the world that He sent His only begotten Son, that whoever believes in him shall not perish but have eternal life.

Continuing with the analogy of a jigsaw puzzle, it may be helpful for us to think of bible passages such as 1 John 4:8 and John 3:16 which speak of God's love as being comparable to the outside pieces of a puzzle. They are the flat-edged pieces we begin with which frame the rest of the puzzle and help us to understand the relationships of the internal pieces. Toward that end, and as a practical exercise, let's consider how John 3:16 could be read if Jesus is not God:

> For God so loved the world that He sent *someone else*, that whoever believes in *someone else* shall not perish but have eternal life.

My paraphrase may have jarred some readers, so let me illustrate the point. Imagine that you are standing in the yard with your son while your daughter plays in her second-floor bedroom, and before long you notice smoke and flames are coming from the kitchen window, and they are quickly spreading throughout the rest of the house. Because of your deep love for your daughter, you exclaim to your son, "Suzie's in danger—go inside and save her!" Without hesitation your son does exactly what you ask and rushes into the blazing house. From your safe vantage point outside, you eventually see that he has made it to her bedroom, and you eagerly wait for them to get out before it's too late.

You are frozen in despair until a lower-level window shatters, and from the thick, black smoke a smoldering bundle is pushed hastily through the opening. You grab your daughter as she struggles to get to safety; unfortunately, the smoke and flames overtake your son and he dies alone inside the house.

After the smoke has cleared and some days have passed, you stand before a gathering of friends and family at the funeral of your beloved son where you declare that your son's heroic and heart-wrenching sacrifice to save his sister is proof of *your* great love!

Questions:

- How does your son's sacrifice to save his sister illustrate how much you love her?
- Why didn't you, the father, sacrifice your life for your daughter and thus spare your son by doing so?
- Does this story illustrate how much you loved your daughter, or how much your son loved his sister?

Metanarrative

I think we can agree that this illustration presents an unsettling dissonance between the love you profess to have for your daughter and the fact that you asked your son to save her instead of saving her yourself. It is certainly true that your son demonstrated love for his sister by saving her; however, his love for her can hardly be construed as evidence of your love for her. What's more, your son's sacrifice for his sister demonstrated loving obedience and sacrifice toward you, his father, which is a further credit to his character, not yours. This much is clear:

- Your son made the ultimate sacrifice; you did not.
- Your son demonstrated consummate love; you did not.
- Your son had skin in the game; you did not.

With this in mind, let's look again at John 3:16 from the JW perspective that Jesus is not God, but is actually someone else.

> For God so loved the world that He sent *someone else*, that whoever believes in *someone else* shall not perish but have eternal life.

Do you recognize the disparity? If Jesus is not God, then John 3:16 really means that God loved us so much that He sent someone else to sacrifice himself for us, but in fact the sacrifice that Jesus made demonstrates how much Jesus loves us, not how much the Father loves us. Thus, this verse is a meaningful statement only if Jesus shares divinity with the Father and is not someone else, because only then does the Father likewise share in the sacrifice for all mankind; only then does this verse reasonably extol the love of the Father for the sacrifice of the Son.

If Jesus is "one with the Father" (Jn 10:30) in fully sharing the divine identity, then the Father didn't send someone else; He sent himself in Jesus Christ—"very God of very God"[2] as the early church affirmed. Therefore, the Father and the Son are not only one in purpose, but one in nature as well, which makes sense of the biblical assertion that the Son's sacrifice is evidence of the Father's love.

No Skin in the Game

To further establish the point, let's consider another well-known bible verse which speaks of love and helps to frame our understanding of the relationship between the Father and the Son:

> Greater love has no one than this, that one lay down his life for his friends. (Jn 15:13, NASB)

Contextually, the apostle John is setting forth Jesus Christ as the paragon of love whom we are supposed to imitate; therefore, according to this verse no one has greater love than Jesus. Consequently, if Jesus is not God then we must square the fact that, in practical terms, Jesus has even greater love for us than God has because God did not lay down His life for us, whereas Jesus did.

Of course, it could be said that John didn't intend to compare Jesus's love to the Father's love; he meant only to demonstrate the prime example of human love. This is unconvincing, however, because it remains peculiar for scripture to laud God for Jesus's prime example of human love. Consider these words from the apostle John:

> Beloved, let us love one another, for love is from God; and everyone who loves is born of God and knows God. The one who does not love does not know God, for God is love. (1 Jn 4:7,8).

So far, so good. John is simply saying that when we love each other we reveal ourselves to be intimately aligned with God, the source of love. Interestingly, this passage continues by commending the supremacy of God's love by appealing to the sacrifice of Jesus Christ:

> God's love was revealed among us in this way: God sent His One and Only Son into the world so that we might live through Him. Love consists in this: not that we loved God, but that He loved us and sent His Son to be the propitiation for our sins. (1 Jn 4:9,10, HCSB)

Metanarrative

Very simply, then, God demonstrated His love for us by providing a sacrifice. Jesus, however, demonstrated his love for us by being the sacrifice, and his sacrifice was unique in one very important respect. Unlike the sacrifice that God provided for Abraham in Isaac's stead on Mount Moriah (which prefigured the sacrifice of Jesus), Jesus was not a ram caught in a thicket (Gen. 22:12-14). He was a willing sacrifice; it was his choice. Had Jesus declined to become the sacrifice in our stead, then God would not have been able to claim him as the sign of His great love. Therefore, Jesus is the fulcrum of our salvation, and Jesus's love for us is of chief importance.

Consider also the words of the apostle Paul to the Romans:

God proves His own love for us in that while we were still sinners, Christ died for us! (Rom. 5:8)

Full stop. How did *God* prove His own love for us? *Christ* died for us. This is a truly remarkable statement.

If Jesus Christ is not God, then this verse is possibly the most glaring non sequitur ever penned. It would be similar to my saying, "I proved how hungry I was in that while I was at the restaurant a Russian cosmonaut ate four hamburgers!" or "The president showed how patriotic he was in that while he was at the parade a veteran in a wheelchair waved a flag." In each of these cases there is no logical connection between the main clause and the subordinate clause—*unless* the president is a wheelchair-bound veteran, *unless* I am a Russian cosmonaut, and *unless* Jesus Christ is God.

The only conceivable way that Romans 5:8 is a coherent and meaningful statement is if Jesus Christ is God; otherwise, the proof of God's love for us is *someone else's* act of love for us. Therefore, let's consider how that verse could be read if Jesus is not one with the Father in fully sharing the divine nature:

But God proves His own love for us in that while we were still sinners, *someone else* died for us!

No Skin in the Game

If Jesus Christ is not God, then we cannot help being struck by the awful incongruity of scripture commending God for Jesus's sacrifice. Lest we forget what Jesus's sacrifice entailed and how it showed that there is no greater love, let's reflect on a few significant details. Recall that Jesus told his disciples that if he wanted, he could have the Father provide some seventy thousand angels to deliver him from his accusers, but he didn't ask for it. Jesus also said,

> [...] the Father loves me, because I lay down my life so that I may take it up again. No one takes it away from me, but I lay it down on my own initiative. I have authority to lay it down, and I have authority to take it up again. (Jn 10:17-18)

Consequently, we know that at any moment during his hours-long torture and crucifixion Jesus could have called it quits. He could have said "it is finished" (Jn 19:30) by abandoning the crucifixion, and we would have remained lost in our sins. It was his choice. Instead, Jesus said to the Father, "not my will, but Yours be done," (Lk 22:42), and in doing so, the Son did what the Father could not do: he sacrificed himself for us.

The Father could not offer himself as the required blood sacrifice for our sins because that sacrifice required a body; it required a Son of Man, whereas God in His natural state is spirit (Jn 4:24). Therefore, the Word became flesh, and the Son "endured the cross, despising the shame" (Heb 12:2, NASB) until God's will was accomplished for our benefit. The Father did not do that, the Son did. And as John 15:13 says, there is no greater love than that.

The passages we've considered thus far fit the biblical metanarrative of God's preeminent love only if Jesus Christ is one with the Father in fully sharing the divine nature. The view of Jesus Christ as fully man and fully God (the Son of Man and the Son of God) affirms the primacy of God's love in the act of His own ultimate sacrifice, because it was God who laid down His life for His friends. That is amazing grace! God didn't send someone else to do the dirty work—the heavy lifting of personal sacrifice and of making a way of return and right standing with Him—He did it Himself. He came to His own (Jn. 1:11), *Immanuel*, who is God with

Metanarrative

us (Is 7:14). This means that God does have skin in the game after all. He is not strangely divested or disturbingly vicarious, claiming credit for another's sacrifice as He stands watching from a distance, for Jesus said, "He who has seen me has seen the Father" (Jn 14:9).

The JW who has been taught to deny the deity of Jesus Christ may secretly admit to himself that it seems odd for God to take credit for Jesus's sacrifice, but because he is deeply devoted to a particular theology (and a particular theological community), he elects to force these pieces of the puzzle together in such a way that fits that theological framework. Unfortunately, he is unable to explain the resulting deficiency in God's character: namely, His love becomes derivative because it has been arrogated from the life, love, and sacrifice of *someone else*.

Of course, it is not merely problematic for the JW that God takes credit for and even frames His own love by appealing to the sacrifice of Jesus; it is principally problematic that God requires someone else die for our sins at all! Philosopher and author Dr. Glenn Peoples has addressed this very problem:

> For God to take a third person—a person who is not God but a bystander—and subject him to death as an atoning sacrifice is unjust. It is akin to me robbing a third party in order to wipe your debt to me rather than paying it myself or absorbing the loss. [...].

> But if Jesus is truly divine, as the Scripture and the Christian faith teach, then things are different, for Jesus is the one against whom we have sinned, and his death is a case of the wronged party choosing to suffer and die so that the wrongdoers can be freed of their burden of debt. This is a case of a self-giving God.[3]

Dr. People's argument enjoys the force of being perfectly self-evident, and I can only add that the unjust nature of having an innocent third party die for all mankind's sins is compounded when God subsequently takes credit for his sacrifice.

Furthermore, though often overlooked, God could have just as well decreed the following:

From any tree of the garden you may eat freely; but from the tree of the knowledge of good and evil you shall not eat, for in the day that you eat from it you will surely ~~die~~ *owe me an apology*. (Gen 2:16, rhetorical paraphrase)

And the apostle Paul could have likewise affirmed the following:

And according to the Law, one may almost say, all things are cleansed with ~~blood~~ *an apology*, and without ~~shedding of blood~~ *an apology* there is no forgiveness. (Heb 9:22, rhetorical paraphrase)

But that's not what happened. God exercised His prerogative to choose the punishment for sin, and He determined that the wages of sin would be death (Rom 6:23, NASB). He demanded that the very life of the sinner be forfeited—*sacrificed*. Even so, God offered the substitutionary sacrifice of one innocent man for us all, which is certainly wonderful, but it is also very disconcerting. The prophet Isaiah described it this way:

Surely our griefs he himself bore, and our sorrows he carried; yet we ourselves esteemed him stricken, smitten of God, and afflicted. But he was pierced through for our transgressions, he was crushed for our iniquities; the chastening for our well-being fell upon him, and by his scourging we are healed. All of us like sheep have gone astray, each of us has turned to his own way; but Jehovah has caused the iniquity of us all to fall on him.

He was oppressed and he was afflicted, yet he did not open his mouth; like a lamb that is led to slaughter, and like a sheep that is silent before its shearers, so he did not open his mouth. By oppression and judgment he was taken away; and as for his generation, who considered that he was cut off out of the land of the living for the transgression of my people, to whom the stroke was due? His grave was assigned with wicked men, yet he was with a rich man in his death, because he had done no violence, nor was there any deceit in his mouth.

Metanarrative

> But the Lord was pleased to crush him, putting him to grief [...].
> (Is 53:4-10)

Jehovah was pleased to crush Jesus for our iniquities. In effect, God said, "I will let all of you guilty sinners off the hook if I can put this one perfectly blameless man on the hook in your place." The injustice inherent in that exchange is obvious. However (and this is crucial), if God Himself is the one who enters into the exchange as the innocent third party, becoming a man readied for sacrifice, then He has taken the injustice upon Himself! This is precisely the beauty of the gospel of Jesus Christ, and it is wholly consistent with the metanarrative that scripture provides of God's consummate and preeminent love for us. God intentionally set the price of our redemption at the cost of His own life, not the life of someone else.

Dr. Peoples sums this up nicely:

> This is the point. The two parties concerned with the problem of sin are God and humanity. Humanity has sinned against God, and these are the two parties that need to be reconciled. What [some] are proposing is that God called on a third party to suffer and die to make this happen, which is unjust, since the third party is not God (the wronged party). The Gospel message is one in which God did for humanity that which we could not do.[4]

Thus far I have given numerous examples of the Father being credited for the sacrificial offering provided by the Son, and I have demonstrated that this is only problematic if the Father and the Son are not one in nature or identity. The very language of these passages presupposes the shared nature of the Father and the Son.

We will now consider the many passages of scripture which effectively turn the tables and give credit to the Son for acts and characteristics that, until the time of Christ, had been attributed only to Jehovah. This will serve to further illuminate the relationship between the Father and the Son.

2. Shared Glory

What's Yours Is Mine, What's Mine Is Yours

> I am Jehovah thy God, who brought thee out of the land of Egypt, out of the house of bondage. Thou shalt have no other gods before me. Thou shalt not make unto thee a graven image, nor any likeness of any thing that is in heaven above, or that is in the earth beneath, or that is in the water under the earth. Thou shalt not bow down thyself unto them, nor serve them, for I Jehovah thy God am a jealous God [...]. (Ex 20:2-5, ASV)

> I am Jehovah, that is my name; and my glory will I not give to another, neither my praise unto graven images. (Is 42:8)

Naturally, passages such as these suggest that we should "ascribe to Yahweh the glory due His name" (Ps 29:2, Ps 96:8, 1 Chron 16:29, HCSB), and as a corollary we should not ascribe to others the honor that is due only to Him. This speaks to the strict monotheism that was required of all Jews in the Old Testament passage of scripture known as the *Shema*:

> Hear, O Israel: Jehovah our God is one Jehovah: and thou shalt love Jehovah thy God with all thy heart, and with all thy soul, and with all thy might. [...] Thou shalt fear Jehovah thy God; and him shalt thou serve, and shalt swear by his name. Ye shall not go after other gods, of the gods of the peoples that are round about you; for Jehovah thy God in the midst of thee is a jealous God; lest the anger of Jehovah thy God be kindled against thee, and he destroy thee from off the face of the earth. (Deut 6:4,5, 13-15)

Shared Glory

Having set the stage, then, let's look at our first example of how Jehovah flips the script, does the unthinkable, and shares His glory with Jesus Christ.

❖ **Shared Creation**

Jehovah is the Creator

> I am Yahweh, who made everything; who stretched out the heavens by Myself; who alone spread out the earth. (Is 44:24, HCSB)

> I [Jehovah] made the earth, and created man on it. It was My hands that stretched out the heavens, and I commanded all their host. (Is 45:12)

> Everyone who is called by My name [Jehovah], And whom I have created for My glory, whom I have formed, even whom I have made. (Is 43:7, NASB)

Jesus Christ is the Creator

> In the beginning was the Word, and the Word was with God, and the Word was God. He was with God in the beginning. All things were created through him, and apart from him not one thing was created that has been created [...]. The Word became flesh and took up residence among us. (Jn 1:1-3, 14, HCSB)

> [Jesus Christ] is the image of the invisible God, the firstborn over all creation. For everything was created by him, in heaven and on earth, the visible and the invisible, whether thrones or dominions or rulers or authorities—all things have been created through him and for him. (Col 1:13-16)

> But of the Son He says, "Your throne, O God, is forever and ever, and the righteous scepter is the scepter of His kingdom. "You have loved righteousness and hated lawlessness; Therefore God, Your God, has anointed You with the oil of gladness above Your companions." And, "You, Lord, in the beginning laid the foundation of the earth, and the heavens are the works of Your hands." (Heb 1:8-10, NASB)

The Old Testament verses just cited declare unequivocally that Jehovah created the heavens and the earth:

- By Himself (Is. 44:24)
- With His own hands (Is. 45:12)
- For His own glory (Is. 43:7)

Yet the New Testament verses just cited declare emphatically that everything was created:

- By Jesus Christ (Col. 1:16)
- By Jesus Christ's own hands (Heb. 1:10)
- Through Jesus Christ (Jn. 1:3, Col. 1:16)
- For Jesus Christ (Col. 1:16)

How should we understand these seemingly disparate claims? Indeed, how would the prophet Malachi understand them?

> Don't all of us have one Father? Didn't one God create us? (Mal 2:10, HCSB)

First of all, we must recognize a basic truth: only God can create ex nihilo or "out of nothing." God creates, whereas creatures procreate. Stated another way, only God can produce, whereas creatures merely reproduce, and only their own kind. It follows logically, then, that only God can create outside of his own kind, which is everyone else and everything else that exists. Therefore, it is significant that scripture declares that Jesus Christ created every thing of every kind, from nothing, in the beginning.

In his widely respected work *Jesus and the God of Israel: God Crucified and Other Studies on the New Testament's Christology of Divine Identity*, Richard Bauckham affirms that creation is the role of God alone while providing valuable insight into the mindset of strictly monotheistic Jews of the Second Temple period:

> [F]or Jewish monotheism, the eternal divine sovereignty, including God's unique creative activity in the beginning as well as his providential ordering of all things and his future completion of his purpose for his reign over all things, is properly indivisible. God alone rules all things and will rule all things because he alone created all things. [...]. The participation of Christ in the creative work of God is necessary, in Jewish monotheistic terms, to complete the otherwise incomplete inclusion of him in the divine identity. It also makes even clearer that the intention of this early Christology is precisely to include him in the unique divine identity, since, in the creative work of God, there was, for Jewish monotheists, no room even for servants of God to carry out his work at his command. Creation, axiomatically, was the sole work of God alone.[5]

Thus, were Jesus Christ a mere created being, there would be no scriptural or rational basis for attributing to him the divine ability to create ex nihilo. Yet, because scripture clearly does attribute this ability to Jesus, we are justified in concluding that he shares the divine identity with the Father.

Let's turn to our next example of Jehovah sharing His glory with Jesus Christ.

❖ **Shared Name**

Jehovah is *the Alpha and the Omega, the First and the Last, the Beginning and the End*

> Who has performed and done this, calling the generations from the beginning? I, Yahweh, am the first, and with the last—I am He. (Is 41:4)

> Thus saith Jehovah, the King of Israel, and his Redeemer, Jehovah of hosts: I am the first, and I am the last; and besides me there is no God. (Is 44:6, ASV)

> Listen to Me, Jacob, and Israel, the one called by Me: I am He; I am the first, I am also the last. (Is 48:12, HCSB)

> "I am the Alpha and the Omega," says the Lord God, "who is and who was and who is to come, the Almighty." (Rev 1:8, NASB)

> And He who sits on the throne said, "Behold, I am making all things new." And He said, "Write, for these words are faithful and true." Then He said to me, "It is done. I am the Alpha and the Omega, the beginning and the end. I will give to the one who thirsts from the spring of the water of life without cost." (Rev 21:5,6)

Jesus Christ is *the Alpha and the Omega, the First and the Last, the Beginning and the End*

> [...] I heard behind me a loud voice like the sound of a trumpet [...]. Then I turned to see the voice that was speaking with me [...]. When I saw Him, I fell at His feet like a dead man. And He placed His right hand on me, saying, "Do not be afraid; I am the first and the last, and the living One; and I was dead, and behold, I am alive forevermore, and I have the keys of death and of Hades. (Rev 1:10,12,17,18)

Shared Glory

> And to the angel of the church in Smyrna write: the first and the last, who was dead, and has come to life, says this [...]. (Rev 2:8)

> Behold, I am coming quickly, and my reward is with me, to render to every man according to what he has done. I am the Alpha and the Omega, the first and the last, the beginning and the end. Blessed are those who wash their robes, so that they may have the right to the tree of life, and may enter by the gates into the city. Outside are the dogs and the sorcerers and the immoral persons and the murderers and the idolaters, and everyone who loves and practices lying. I, Jesus, have sent my angel to testify to you these things for the churches. I am the root and the descendant of David, the bright morning star. (Rev 22:12-16)

It is clear from the verses just cited that Jehovah and Jesus Christ share the designations of *the Alpha and the Omega, the First and the Last, the Beginning and the End*. Since there cannot be two firsts and two lasts it is reasonable to conclude that, in the same way Jehovah and Jesus Christ share the credit and the glory for creating everything, they likewise share the credit and the glory for being *the Alpha and the Omega, the First and the Last, the Beginning and the End* in relation to what they created, but this can only be true if they (plural) are one (singular) in some intrinsic sense, because Jehovah avowed that He will not share His glory with someone else. Richard Baukham comments on the importance of these shared titles:

> They say something significant about [the book of Revelation's] inclusion of Jesus in the unique divine identity.
> In the form, "the first and the last," the title comes from Deutero-Isaiah [Isaiah chapters 40—55], where it is one of the terms that encapsulates Deutero-Isaianic monotheism. It expresses the unique eternal sovereignty of the one God, who precedes all things as their Creator, and as the Lord of history brings all things to their escha-

tological fulfilment. He is the source and the goal of all things. Revelation thus includes Christ both protologically and eschatologically in the identity of the one God of Deutero-Isaianic monotheism.[6]

Another striking example of Jehovah sharing His glory with Jesus Christ with respect to His name is seen in Paul's letter to the Romans:

Jehovah's Name Saves

And it shall be that whosoever shall call upon the name of Jehovah shall be saved. (Joel 2:32, DARBY, public domain)

Jesus Christ's Name Saves

If you confess with your mouth Jesus as Lord, and believe in your heart that God raised Him from the dead, you will be saved; for with the heart a person believes, resulting in righteousness, and with the mouth he confesses, resulting in salvation. For the Scripture says, "Whoever believes in Him will not be disappointed." For there is no distinction between Jew and Greek; for the same Lord is Lord of all, abounding in riches for all who call on Him; for "Whoever calls on the name of the Lord will be saved." (Rom 10:9-13, NASB)

In this passage, Paul is clearly quoting Joel 2:32, an Old Testament verse explicitly about Jehovah, but he replaces the name *Jehovah* with the title *Lord*, and he plainly applies the text to Jesus Christ. It is certain that Paul, a faithful monotheist, would not do such a thing unless he believed that Jesus Christ is God.

It is important to note that in all of the more than five thousand existing Greek manuscripts of the New Testament, there is not a single instance where the author used the divine name *Jehovah*, even when an Old Testament Hebrew passage being quoted originally used the divine name (such as Joel 2:32). The designation *Lord* (*Kyrios*) is always used instead of *Jehovah*, effectively revealing the New Testament author's understanding of the nature of Jesus Christ by including him in the unique identity of Jehovah.

The significance of the designation *Lord* being used instead of the divine name may be lost on the rank and file JW because the anonymous authors of their *New World Translation* of the bible have summarily excised *Lord* and inserted *Jehovah* into the text 237 times despite there being no manuscript evidence that *Jehovah* was ever used by the original authors of the New Testament.

In his compelling work, *The Tetragrammaton and the Christian Greek Scriptures,* Lynn Lundquist affirms that the JW's have no scriptural or historical warrant for making such a revision:

> In summary of our search of Greek manuscripts and surrounding historical data, we conclude that no evidence exists indicating that the Tetragrammaton was used by the inspired writers of the Greek Scriptures [i.e. the New Testament]. To bring the Tetragrammaton into the Christian Scriptures requires that we deny the inspiration and authority of the Greek Scriptures themselves and seek a higher authority in Hebrew translations [i.e. later Hebrew translations of the original Greek/Aramaic New Testament scriptures].[7]

Let's move on to a similar example in which Jehovah shares His glory with Jesus Christ, which is found in Paul's letter to the Philippians:

Every Knee Bows to Jehovah

> Who announced it from ancient times? Was it not I, Yahweh? There is no other God but Me, a righteous God and Savior; there is no one except Me. Turn to Me and be saved, all the ends of the earth. For I am God, and there is no other. By Myself I have sworn; Truth has gone from My mouth, a word that will not be revoked: Every knee will bow to Me, every tongue will swear allegiance. (Is 45:21-23, HCSB)

No Skin in the Game

Every Knee Bows to Jesus Christ

> For this reason also, God highly exalted Him, and bestowed on Him the name which is above every name, so that at the name of Jesus every knee will bow, of those who are in heaven and on earth and under the earth, and that every tongue will confess that Jesus Christ is Lord, to the glory of God the Father. (Phil 2:9-11, NASB)

Paul declares that the name which everyone will bow to is Jesus Christ, not Jehovah, in contradistinction to Isaiah 45:23. Remember that in all of the extant Greek New Testament manuscripts there is not a single instance of the name *Jehovah* being used. From the book of Matthew to the book of Revelation the name which is exalted is Jesus Christ. Jesus Christ is *Lord*. We must ask, therefore, how this squares with the fact that Jehovah said He will not share His glory with someone else.

It is also noteworthy that while Paul equates Jesus Christ with Jehovah, he retains the distinction between Jesus Christ the Son and God the Father (v10). Again, we see that scripture suggests that there is somehow a singularity and a plurality in the nature of Jehovah (see Gen 1:26). The historical Christian view is that the Father shares His glory with the Son and this does not contradict Jehovah's edict that He will not share His glory with another because Jesus Christ is not another; he is not *someone else*. He is one with the Father in nature and is included in the identity of God. We will discuss later how this can be, but for the time being let us consider the next example of Jehovah sharing His glory with Jesus Christ.

❖ **Shared Judgment**

Jehovah Judges

> Ascribe to Yahweh the glory of His name; bring an offering and enter His courts. Worship the Lord in the splendor of His holiness; tremble before Him, all the earth. Say among the nations: "The Lord reigns. The world is firmly established; it cannot be shaken. He judges the peoples fairly." Let the heav-

ens be glad and the earth rejoice; let the sea and all that fills it resound. Let the fields and everything in them exult. Then all the trees of the forest will shout for joy before the Lord, for He is coming—for He is coming to judge the earth. (Ps 96:8-13, HCSB)

Let the fields and everything in them exult. Then all the trees of the forest will shout for joy before Jehovah, for He is coming—for He is coming to judge the earth. He will judge the world with righteousness and the peoples with His faithfulness. (Ps 96:12,13)

For God will bring every act to judgment, including every hidden thing, whether good or evil. (Eccl 12:14)

Jesus Christ Judges

The Father, in fact, judges no one but has given all judgment to the Son, so that all people will honor the Son just as they honor the Father. Anyone who does not honor the Son does not honor the Father who sent Him. (Jn 5:22,23)

For just as the Father has life in Himself, so also He has granted to the Son to have life in Himself. And He has granted Him the right to pass judgment, because He is the Son of Man. (Jn 5:26,27)

I solemnly charge you before God and Christ Jesus, who is going to judge the living and the dead, and because of His appearing and His kingdom. (2 Tim 4:1)

In the Old Testament passages just cited, we are told that Jehovah will come to judge the earth, but then the apostle John asserts that the Father "has given all judgment to the Son." God has abdicated all judgment to Jesus "because he is the Son of Man" (Jn 5:27). Why would He abdicate all judgment to a son of man? Evidently there are some missing pieces of our puzzle which must be filled in to provide a clearer picture of Jesus Christ as the Son of Man and what that means about his relationship to God.

Numerous other examples could be given to illustrate that Jehovah shares His glory with Jesus Christ, such as the sharing of judgment in the "Judgment Seat of God" and the "Judgment Seat of Christ," or again in "The Day of Jehovah" and "The Day of the Lord"/"The Day of Christ," but we don't need to belabor the point any further.

We have seen that Jehovah shares the credit and the glory with Jesus Christ as Creator, as Judge, and in the honor given to his name, and I have provided what I think is a fair explanation of how these facts harmonize with the doctrine of the deity of Jesus Christ. I have also shown that these facts are incongruous with the biblical metanarrative of God's preeminent love if Jesus Christ is not God. We will now explore God's purpose for uniting the functions of the Son of God and the Son of Man in the person of the Messiah.

3. Mediating Messiah

The Son of God + the Son of Man

The author of the book of Hebrews used many Old Testament texts to show that the Messiah was prophesied to be the perfect high priest who would sacrifice himself once for all, unlike the high priests of Israel who performed daily sacrifices for themselves and the rest of the people. In doing so, the Messiah must be a sinless son of man to fulfill his role as the unblemished, atoning sacrifice—thus making this son of man *the* Son of Man.

> For it was fitting for us to have such a high priest, holy, innocent, undefiled, separated from sinners and exalted above the heavens; who does not need daily, like those high priests, to offer up sacrifices, first for His own sins and then for the sins of the people, because this He did once for all when He offered up Himself. […].
>
> For the Law, since it is only a shadow of the good things to come and not the very form of things, can never, by the same sacrifices which they offer continually year by year, make perfect those who draw near. Otherwise, would they not have ceased to be offered, because the worshipers, having once been cleansed, would no longer have had consciousness of sins? But in those sacrifices there is a reminder of sins year by year. For it is impossible for the blood of bulls and goats to take away sins.
>
> Therefore, when he comes into the world, he says, "Sacrifice and offering You have not desired, but a body You have prepared for me; in whole burnt offerings and sacrifices for sin You have taken

Mediating Messiah

no pleasure. "Then I said, 'Behold, I have come (In the scroll of the book it is written of me) to do Your will, O God.'"

After saying above, "Sacrifices and offerings and whole burnt offerings and sacrifices for sin You have not desired, nor have You taken pleasure in them" (which are offered according to the Law), then He said, "Behold, I have come to do Your will." He takes away the first in order to establish the second. By this will we have been sanctified through the offering of the body of Jesus Christ once for all. (Heb 7:26,27,10:1-10, NASB)

Jesus fulfilled the necessary condition of being a sinless son of man to offer his high priestly sacrifice. However, while sinlessness was a necessary condition to provide an acceptable sacrifice, it was not a sufficient condition because scripture states variously that no man can redeem another man, and only God can be savior with respect to man's sin:

No man can by any means redeem his brother or give to God a ransom for him, for the redemption of his soul is costly [...]. (Ps 49:7,8)

I, even I, am Jehovah; and besides me there is no saviour. (Is 43:11, ASV)

Yet I am Jehovah thy God from the land of Egypt; and thou shalt know no god but me, and besides me there is no saviour. (Hos 13:4)

Consequently, while it is true that the Messiah had to be a perfect man, he had to be more than a perfect man because that was not enough for atonement. Richard Bauckham provides valuable insight into another condition the Messiah had to satisfy:

[In] Hebrews, the atoning work of Christ follows broadly the pattern of the Levitical high priest's activity. Jesus offers himself as the atoning sacrifice, then, taking his own sacrificial blood, he enters the heavenly presence of God and comes before God's throne, just as the high priest entered the inner sanctuary on earth on the Day of Atonement and sprinkled the blood of the sacrifice before the ark of the covenant. Where the two part company, however, is when Jesus sits down on the throne. Not only did the Levitical high priest not do this; it would, of course, have been unthinkable for him to have done so.

Hebrews clearly sees this difference in terms of the finality and permanence of Christ's atoning sacrifice. He has no need, like the Levitical high priests, to return to the people and repeat the ceremony year by year. Thus, according to 10:12, when he "had offered for all time a single sacrifice for sins, he sat down at the right hand of God." But the point cannot be simply that, having made the once-and-for-all, finally adequate sacrifice for all sins, he stays in the heavenly sanctuary, nor even that he stays in order continually to intercede for his people on the basis of his sacrifice (7:25). For these purposes, it would be sufficient for him to stand in the presence of God, as all the angels do. The potent imagery of sitting on the cosmic throne has only one attested significance: it indicates his participation in the unique sovereignty of God over the world. That Jesus sits on the throne, not only as king but also as high priest (which Hebrews clearly indicates), indicates surely that his completed work of atonement is now permanently part of the divine rule over the world. In this way, *this* high priesthood, unlike the Levitical, does belong to the unique identity of God. *This high priest is the perfect mediator; he not only represents his people to God, in sacrifice and intercession, but also embodies the grace and mercy of God to which his sacrifice now gives permanent expression.*[8]

In other words, the Messiah must also be a particular kind of mediator between God and man; to be specific, he must fully represent both parties involved, not just one:

Mediating Messiah

Now a mediator is not for one party only; whereas God is only one. (Gal 3:20, NASB)

As mediator, the Messiah must represent God in His requirement for holiness and justice, and he must represent man in his appeal for mercy and forgiveness. This need of man was insightfully, if curiously, expressed by Eli in the book of 1 Samuel:

If one man sins against another, God will mediate for him; but if a man sins against the Lord, who can intercede for him? (1 Sam 2:25)

Evidently, Eli reasoned that because God was squarely on the transgressed side of the offense—opposite his transgressor—He would not represent both Himself and his transgressor with respect to the offense. Although Eli clearly saw that there was a need for a mediator between God and man, he was wrong to surmise that God would not make such a provision. Indeed, while many prophets saw Jesus's day from afar (Jn 8:56, Mt 13:16,17), we are told that Eli's "eyes were set so that he could not see" (1 Sam 4:15), a physical condition which reflected his spiritual condition.

Job also lamented the absence of a mediator between God and man, albeit from the perspective of someone greatly esteemed by God (unlike Eli):

[God is] not a man like me, so that I can answer him, or that we can enter into litigation with one another. There is not yet a mediator between us [God and man], who would set his hand on the two of us. (Job 9:32,33, ISV)

That is, not until Jesus Christ.

As mediator, Jesus had to represent God to man, and he had to represent man to God. But who can represent God? A mere man—even a sinless man—cannot set his hand on the God who "dwells in unapproachable light" (1 Tim 6:16, NASB). The only one who can is God Himself, and this is exactly what we find in Jesus Christ. Jesus had to be the perfect Son of

Man, representing man, and he had to be the holy Son of God, representing God.

The Messiah had to unite the roles of the Son of Man and the Son of God as Jesus indicated in Matthew 16:15-17, and this is the revelation that the Father gave to Peter: Jesus Christ is no mere prophet, no mere son of man, and no mere son of God. As the Messiah, Jesus is the mediator who can set his hand on both God and man because he is both God and man. He fully represents both. Jesus lived perfectly as a sinless son of man, and he was the visible, physical manifestation of the invisible, incorporeal God, come near to mortally fallen men who desperately needed Him to bridge the chasm which separated them. This is why we find such language throughout scripture that entwines both aspects of the Son of Man, *as man*, and the Son of God, *as God*, in the singular person of Jesus Christ. For example:

> He [Jesus Christ] is the image of the invisible God, the firstborn over all creation. For everything was created by Him, in heaven and on earth, the visible and the invisible, whether thrones or dominions or rulers or authorities—all things have been created through Him and for Him. He is before all things, and by Him all things hold together. He is also the head of the body, the church; He is the beginning, the firstborn from the dead, so that He might come to have first place in everything. For God was pleased to have all His fullness dwell in Him, and through Him to reconcile everything to Himself by making peace through the blood of His cross—whether things on earth or things in heaven. (Col 1:16-20, HCSB)

Likewise:

> God, after He spoke long ago to the fathers in the prophets in many portions and in many ways, in these last days has spoken to us in His Son, whom He appointed heir of all things, through whom also He made the world. And He is the radiance of His glory and the exact representation of His nature, and upholds all things by the

word of His power. When He had made purification of sins, He sat down at the right hand of the Majesty on high, having become as much better than the angels, as He has inherited a more excellent name than they. (Heb 1:1-4)

Accordingly, Jesus Christ is the unique Son of Man, fully human in every respect (Heb 2:7), and he is the unique Son of God, fully God in every respect (Col 2:9); uniting in himself the defining characteristics of God and man, and as mediator he represents both of them fully.

Recall as well what the author of the book of Hebrews wrote:

For when God made the promise to Abraham, since He could swear by no one greater, He swore by Himself. (Heb 6:13, NASB)

What God did in that moment is instructive and we should not miss its significance. He considered His covenant with Abraham to be of such supreme importance that He would not seal it with reference to anything or anyone other than Himself—not even an angel. Therefore, He swore by Himself.

Since God considered that His covenant promise to Abraham required such significant treatment at its initiation, we must surely conclude that He would not treat it with diminished significance at its culmination in the sacrifice of Jesus Christ ("the Seed to whom the promise was made" Gal 3:19, HCSB).

It is certainly implausible that God would initiate this covenant by emphatically offering Himself as its seminal and singular guarantor, swearing by Himself, only to bring it to completion by having *someone else*—a mere created being—become the conclusive guarantor of that better covenant. The apostle Paul frames the importance of this covenant for us:

Brothers, I'm using a human illustration. No one sets aside or makes additions to even a human covenant that has been ratified. Now the promises were spoken to Abraham and to his seed. He does not say "and to seeds," as though referring to many, but referring to one, and to your seed, who is Christ. And I say this: The law, which came 430 years later, does not revoke a covenant that was previously ratified by God and cancel the promise. (Gal 3:15-17)

What we have, then, is another vital aspect in which Jehovah shares His glory with Jesus Christ:

Jesus has become the guarantor of a better covenant. (Heb 7:22, ISV)

Both Jehovah and Jesus Christ guarantee the covenant: Jehovah is the sworn guarantor at its inception, and Jesus is the guarantor at its culmination. Of course, if Jesus is Jehovah (along with the Father and the Holy Spirit), then it is a distinction without a difference. In both cases God guarantees the covenant. In the words of Richard Bauckham:

Hebrews portrays Jesus as both truly God and truly human, like his Father in every respect and like humans in every respect. The most fundamental category is that of the Son of God who shares eternally the unique identity of his Father, the unique identity of the God of Israel and the God of all reality. But sonship to God also characterizes Jesus' human solidarity with his fellow-humans. His mission in incarnation was to bring many human sons and daughters of God to glory (2:10-12). Thus sonship in Hebrews is both a divinely exclusive category (Jesus' unique relationship with the Father) and a humanly inclusive category (a form of relationship to the Father that Jesus shares with those he redeems). As the eternally pre-existent Son of God, Jesus Christ is destined and qualified for the two main roles in God's eschatological activity of salvation. Because he is the unique Son of the Father, appointed heir of all things (1:2), he can exercise God's eschatological rule over all things as Lord, and he can make full atonement for sins as the heavenly high priest. But, in both cases, he must also be fully human.[9]

4. The Divine Likeness of Jesus Christ

We have seen that a pattern of shared identity emerges when we mind the biblical metanarrative of God's preeminent love, which culminates in the person and sacrifice of Jesus Christ. C.S. Lewis comments on this recurring pattern of divine likeness:

What are we to make of Jesus Christ? [...].

When you look into His conversation you will find this sort of claim running through the whole thing. For instance, He went about saying to people, "I forgive your sins." Now it is quite natural for a man to forgive something you do to him. Thus if somebody cheats me out of £5 it is quite possible and reasonable for me to say, "Well, I forgive him, we will say no more about it." What on earth would you say if somebody had done you out of £5 and I said, "That is all right, I forgive him"?

Then there is the curious thing which seems to slip out almost by accident. On one occasion this Man is sitting looking down on Jerusalem from the hill above it and suddenly in comes an extraordinary remark—"I keep on sending you prophets and wise men." Nobody comments on it. And yet, quite suddenly, almost incidentally, He is claiming to be the power that all through the centuries is sending wise men and leaders into the world.

Here is another curious remark: in almost every religion there are unpleasant observances like fasting. This Man suddenly remarks one day, "No one need fast while I am here." Who is this Man who remarks that His mere presence suspends all normal rules? [10]

The Divine Likeness of Jesus Christ

We can add to Lewis's observations that Jesus did not sound like any of the messengers of God recorded in scripture, whether prophet or angel. The prophets always deferred to God and exhorted people to believe in Him, whereas Jesus insisted that they have faith in both God and himself. For example:

> Believe in God; believe also in Me. In My Father's house are many dwelling places; if not, I would have told you. I am going away to prepare a place for you. If I go away and prepare a place for you, I will come back and receive you to Myself, so that where I am you may be also. You know the way to where I am going."
>
> "Lord," Thomas said, "we don't know where You're going. How can we know the way?"
>
> Jesus told him, "I am the way, the truth, and the life. No one comes to the Father except through Me.
> "If you know Me, you will also know My Father. From now on you do know Him and have seen Him."
>
> "Lord," said Philip, "show us the Father, and that's enough for us."
>
> Jesus said to him, "Have I been among you all this time without your knowing Me, Philip? The one who has seen Me has seen the Father. How can you say, 'Show us the Father'? Don't you believe that I am in the Father and the Father is in Me? (Jn 14:1-10)

Similarly, the angels always deferred to God, adamantly refusing anything remotely resembling worship, including the prohibition of bowing down to them, but Jesus accepted all manner of worship readily. In fact, the apostle John describes this vision at the throne of God:

> Then I looked, and I heard the voice of many angels around the throne and the living creatures and the elders; and the number of them was myriads of myriads, and thousands of thousands, saying

with a loud voice, "Worthy is the Lamb that was slain to receive power and riches and wisdom and might and honor and glory and blessing." And every created thing which is in heaven and on the earth and under the earth and on the sea, and all things in them, I heard saying, "To Him who sits on the throne, and to the Lamb, be blessing and honor and glory and dominion forever and ever." And the four living creatures kept saying, "Amen." And the elders fell down and worshiped. (Rev 5:11-14, NASB)

Richard Bauckham expounds on the explicit worship being given to Jesus Christ in this passage:

In Philippians 2:9-11 and Revelation 5:13, there are strikingly similar accounts of the worship of Christ by all creation. Philippians 2:10-11 echoes Isaiah 45:23 ("To me every knee shall bow, every tongue shall swear"), but expands the "every knee ... every tongue" of Isaiah, emphasizing the universality of the worship given to Christ with a formula encompassing the whole creation: "every knee shall bow, in heaven and on earth and under the earth" (Phil. 2:10). Revelation 5, having portrayed the exalted Christ as the Lamb in the midst of the divine throne in heaven (5:6; cf. 7:17), includes the Lamb in the worship of God on his throne in heaven, and then expands the circle of worship to include the whole creation: every creature in heaven and on earth and under the earth and in the sea, and all that is in them, singing, "To the one who is seated on the throne and to the Lamb be blessing and honor and glory and might forever and ever!" (Rev. 5:13). It may not be accidental that these formulae for the whole cosmos have one of their closest parallels in the second commandment of the Decalogue (Exod. 20:4; Deut. 5:8-9; cf. also Neh. 9:6, Ps. 146:6; Rev. 10:6, which lack "under the earth"): all those creatures whom it is forbidden to worship are depicted as themselves giving the worship due to God alone to Christ who shares his throne. [...].

The Divine Likeness of Jesus Christ

Revelation portrays the worship of Christ in heaven quite explicitly as *divine* worship (5:8-12). The heavenly worship of God the Creator (4:9-11) is followed by the heavenly worship of the Lamb (5:8-12), and then, as the climax of the vision (5:13), the circle of worship expands to include the whole of creation addressing a doxology to God and the Lamb together. This very deliberate portrayal of the worship of Christ is noteworthy, not only because it occurs in a work whose thought-world is unquestionably thoroughly Jewish, but also because John shows himself quite aware of the issue of *monotheistic* worship. The whole book is much concerned with the question of true and false worship, with differentiating the true worship of God from the idolatrous worship of the beast.[11]

Indeed, the tenor of the entire New Testament is that Jesus Christ shares the glory of Jehovah. Yes, he is the Son of Man; yes, he is the Son of God; and yes, he is Creator, Judge, Lord, and God. It is written all over the New Testament, and often in the most mundane fashion. For example, consider what Jesus said to the religious people of his day:

> You search the Scriptures because you think that in them you have eternal life; it is these that testify about me, and you are unwilling to come to me so that you may have life. (Jn 5:39,40)

Why didn't Jesus say the following instead?

> You search the Scriptures because you think in them you have eternal life; it is these that testify about ~~me~~ *Jehovah*; and you are unwilling to come to ~~me~~ *Jehovah* so that you may have life.

Instead, Jesus said the Scriptures point to him and that people should come to him. No prophet of Israel had the chutzpah to speak so arrogantly of himself before God. That kind of talk was more fitting for the delusional likes of a Pharaoh or a Nebuchadnezzar, who received judgment for their hubris. But Jesus was no mere prophet and no mere king. Only he could say the following:

> Come to me, all of you who are weary and burdened, and I will give you rest. All of you, take up my yoke and learn from me, because I am gentle and humble in heart, and you will find rest for yourselves. For my yoke is easy and my burden is light. (Mt 11:28-30, HCSB)

Consider also Jesus's words to Martha:

> Then Martha said to Jesus, "Lord, if you had been here, my brother wouldn't have died. Yet even now I know that whatever you ask from God, God will give you."
>
> "Your brother will rise again," Jesus told her.
>
> Martha said, "I know that he will rise again in the resurrection at the last day."
>
> Jesus said to her, "I am the resurrection and the life. The one who believes in me, even if he dies, will live. Everyone who lives and believes in me will never die—ever. Do you believe this?"
>
> "Yes, Lord," she told Him, "I believe you are the Messiah, the Son of God, who comes into the world." (Jn 11:21-27)

Martha believed that God would raise Lazarus from the dead if Jesus only asked Him, and yet Jesus did not reply with agreement. Instead, he replied that *he* is the resurrection and the life, and that *in him* is found eternal life. Apparently, he didn't need to ask God. Instead of deferring to God, Jesus claimed to be the agent of resurrection and the source of eternal life.

Remember as well that on the same day of Jesus's resurrection how he joined two of his disciples on the road to Emmaus and encouraged them:

> [...] "O foolish men and slow of heart to believe in all that the prophets have spoken! Was it not necessary for the Christ to suffer these things and to enter into His glory?" Then beginning with Moses and with all the prophets, He explained to them the things concerning Himself in all the Scriptures. (Lk 24:25-27, NASB)

What a sermon that must have been! Starting with Moses and all the prophets, Jesus explained to them all the things "concerning himself" in all the scriptures. Jesus is the central figure in all of prophetic scripture. Even John the Baptist, whom Jesus declared to be the greatest of all the prophets, said this about him:

> I baptize you with water for repentance, but He who is coming after me is mightier than I, and I am not fit to remove His sandals; He will baptize you with the Holy Spirit and fire. (Mt 3:11,12)

No prophet ever spoke this way of another prophet. Jesus Christ is greatly exalted by the prophets, and in the gospels Jesus shamelessly accrues to himself honor and glory, even the honor and glory that is due to God alone. In the words of Ravi Zacharias:

> The name of Christ has been virtually unique and unparalleled in history as the one who claimed in himself to be the locus and the sum and substance of the answer, not only in what he said or what he taught, but in himself, so that if you removed Christ from the gospels there is no gospel message left. He is the central feature of his own message.[12]

Both/And vs. Either/Or

The JW's failure to recognize the deity of Jesus Christ lies partly in how they interpret passages of scripture which highlight the distinctions made between the Father and the Son and conclude that these distinctions are proof that Jesus cannot be God. They find it difficult to appreciate how

No Skin in the Game

Jesus can be created and eternal, how he can die and be immortal, and how he can be man and God at the same time. They have, essentially, an either/or approach to the identity of Jesus Christ. When one passage highlights Jesus's humanity and another passage highlights his divinity, the JW concludes that the humanity passage moderates the divinity passage. They do not allow for a harmonization which is afforded by a both/and view of the nature of Jesus Christ. There are, however, very good reasons for having such a view. John Stott sheds light on the language in scripture which combines Jesus's self-effacing humility and his uniquely audacious identification with God. I quote him at length:

> You know, nothing is more disturbing about Jesus of Nazareth than the egocentricity of his claims and the prominence of the personal pronoun in his teaching. He was, in fact, always teaching about himself, and although it is true he announced the arrival of the Kingdom of God, it was only by adding that he was the person who had come to inaugurate that kingdom. It is also true that he spoke of the Fatherhood of God, but only adding that he was the Father's unique Son.
>
> I find it helpful in my own thinking to summarize the claims of Jesus under three words. The first is the word "fulfillment." You probably know that the first recorded words in the public ministry of Jesus according to the record of Mark are, in the Greek: *peplerotai*, "fulfilled" is the time. The kingdom of God has drawn near; repent and believe the good news. And when a little later he went into the synagogue in Nazareth, the village in which he'd been brought up, and he was given the scroll of the prophecy of Isaiah to read, and he found what in our books is chapter sixty-one, and he started to read, "the spirit of The Lord is upon me because He's anointed me," et cetera; when he finished and wound up the scroll and gave it back to the synagogue attendant and sat down he began to say, "Verily I say unto you this day this scripture 'peplerotai': has been fulfilled in your ears." In other words, if you want to know who Isaiah was writing about, he was writing about me.

The Divine Likeness of Jesus Christ

And so Jesus continued to affirm, "Abraham," he said, "rejoiced to see my day." "Moses wrote about me." And he expounded unto them all the scriptures the things concerning himself. On one occasion he said, "Blessed are your eyes for they see and your ears for they hear, because I tell you," he went on, "many prophets and wise men wanted to see what you see and did not see it, and wanted to hear what you hear and didn't hear it." In other words, they were living in the age of anticipation and you are living in the age of fulfillment. Your eyes are actually seeing and your ears are hearing what had been spoken about for centuries in the prophets. In other words, in Jesus's own estimation of himself, he was not another prophet. Though there are many people prepared to concede he was a prophet, he was not, he said, one more prophet in the endless succession of the centuries; on the contrary, he was the fulfillment of all prophecy and the converging streams of prophecy; all found their climax and conclusion in himself. It was in and with his coming that the kingdom of God had arrived. The word "fulfillment."

And then the second word is the word "intimacy." Jesus claimed a relationship of intimacy with the Father which was shared by no other being. We have to admit that the title 'Son of God' in itself is by no means conclusive. "Son of God" is used, and "daughter of God," too, of a number of people in the Bible. Angels are called sons of God, Adam was called the son of God, so was Solomon and other kings, and the children of Israel. So the title is not conclusive, but the way in which Jesus used it does seem to be, because he added the definite article. He said, "Nobody knows *the* Son except *the* Father, and nobody knows *the* Father except *the* Son, and he to whomsoever the Son chooses to reveal Him." In other words, there existed between the one he called "The Father" and himself a unique reciprocal relationship, and nobody knew the one but the other. This word "intimacy" of relationship.

And then the third word that impresses me is the word "authority." Jesus's contemporaries were utterly astonished by the authority with which he spoke. He was quite unlike the scribes who never taught without quoting their authorities. Jesus didn't quote any authorities but his own. Jesus didn't hide behind another authority; he said, "I say to you," and that was his favorite formula. But in addition to teaching with authority he claimed authority to forgive sins. And when people heard him they raised their eyebrows and said, "But who is this? Who can forgive sins except God only?" To which we reply, "Exactly. Who can?"

And then in addition to authority to teach and authority to forgive was his claimed authority to judge the world. Jesus said on several occasions that he would return at the end of history, that he would sit on the throne of his glory, that all the nations would parade and be assembled before him and that he would proceed to separate them from one another as a shepherd separates sheep from goats. In other words, he held in his hand their eternal destiny. He made himself the central figure on the judgment day.

Now these claims of Jesus: to fulfill prophecy, to know God, to forgive sins, and to judge the world, are so outrageous that we inevitably begin to question his sanity, whether his mind was deranged and whether perhaps he had a fixed delusion about himself. But Jesus of Nazareth showed no signs of imbalance; there was no trace in him of the fanatic, still less the psychotic. On the contrary, he comes before us in the pages of the gospels as the most sane and balanced of human beings. And even those who reject his claims admire his character.

He made himself the central figure on the judgment day and then got on his hands and knees and washed his apostle's feet. Their Lord and their Judge became their servant, and I want to suggest to you that that is not only beautiful but it is also unique. There have, of course, been many self-centered religious leaders down the ages, but they have all behaved like it. There have also been very humble people, but they didn't make the claims that Jesus made. It is, you see, the combination of authority and humility, of self-centered claims and unself-centered character, which we say is unique in the whole history of the world.[13]

Authority and humility. The Son of God and the Son of Man. Jesus humbly deferred to his Father on numerous occasions saying things like, "the Father is greater than I" (Jn 14:28), and "Why do you call me good? No one is good except God alone" (Mk 10:18)[14], which reflected his position of humility as the Son of Man. Conversely, Jesus authoritatively declared, "Whoever has seen me has seen the Father" (Jn 14:9, ESV), "before Abraham was, I am" (Jn 8:58), "I am the resurrection and the life" (Jn 11:25), "I am the bread of life" (Jn 6:35), "I am the door" (Jn 10:9), and "I send you prophets and wise men" (Mt 23:34), which reflected his position of authority as the Son of God.

What are we to make of this recurring pattern of divine likeness respecting Jesus Christ and Almighty God in terms of agency and honor? Is the biblical language just so sloppy and imprecise that it lends itself to wrongly equating the Eternal God with a merely human savior, or did God fill His word with ample confirmation that Jesus Christ is both God and man, the perfect mediator between God and man?

In view of everything previously discussed, I submit that we have overwhelming scriptural warrant to believe that Jesus Christ is identified as God, primarily evidenced by the following:

- Scripture repeatedly assigns to the Father the credit and the glory for the Son's sacrifice—even to the extent of defining God's love by particular appeal to the sacrifice of Jesus Christ.

- Scripture repeatedly assigns to Jesus Christ the credit and the glory that's due only to Jehovah as Creator, as Judge, and in the honor given to his name—even to the extent of receiving worship from men and angels.

No Skin in the Game

- New Testament authors quote numerous Old Testament passages that explicitly refer to Jehovah and apply them—without qualification—to Jesus Christ.

- Scripture repeatedly portrays the Messiah as the perfect mediator between God and Man, overtly recognizing him as *the* Son of God and *the* Son of Man, fully representing both natures in his singular being.

- Scripture portrays Jesus Christ, a wholly innocent man, as God's substitutionary sacrifice for sinners, which is plainly unjust if Jesus doesn't share the identity of God.

When Jesus Christ is understood to be God, all of these "converging streams" in scripture come together to form a coherent picture which fits perfectly the biblical metanarrative of God's preeminent love for all humanity. However, when Jesus Christ is not understood to be God, the biblical metanarrative becomes fatally fragmented because God's love is then conspicuously derived from the person and work of Jesus Christ.

In view of a fair reckoning of the whole of scripture and with the big picture squarely before us, the God of the Jehovah's Witness is seen to have no skin in the game in every sense of the term. He is far removed from the shared pathos of man, and he is equally detached from the passion of Jesus Christ. In the final analysis, the gospel of Jesus Christ as portrayed by the Jehovah's Witness is the good news of *someone else*, which is not good news at all considering all of its requisite implications. But there remains good news for the Jehovah's Witness.

I began this endeavor by saying that it is possible for us to honor or dishonor God by the things we believe about Him, and that our image of God must fit the biblical metanarrative for all to be well with our souls. Jesus asked his disciples the most crucial question: "Who do you say that I am?" He asks us the same today.

> We have redemption in Him through His blood, the forgiveness of our trespasses, according to the riches of His grace that He lav-

ished on us with all wisdom and understanding. He made known to us the mystery of His will, according to His good pleasure that He planned in Him for the administration of the days of fulfillment—to bring everything together in the Messiah, both things in heaven and things on earth in Him. (Eph. 1:7-10)

5. Appendix

God: In Person and in Being

Those of us who embrace the orthodox Trinitarian view must explain how we can reasonably believe that:

- The One God, Jehovah, is comprised of multiple persons.
- The One God, Jehovah, is comprised of both uncreated God and created man at the same time.

Certainly the JWs are correct to say that these are insurmountable obstacles to belief in the deity of Jesus Christ; are they not? Absolutely not. Let me explain.

JW's are taught to deny the commonly accepted, scholarly translation of John 1:1 which reads as follows:

In the beginning was the Word, and the Word was with God, and the Word was God.

According to an orthodox understanding, this passage teaches that the Word is and always has been God, and that he entered into our world as Jesus Christ. However, the JWs have reinterpreted John 1:1 in their anonymously translated *New World Translation* of the bible to read "and the word was [a] god," because they contend that the concept of God as a Trinity is logically inconsistent. Therefore, they question, "how can an individual be *with* someone and at the same time be that person?" [15] Let's clear up the confusion.

Singular Being, Plurality of Persons

Is it possible for one being to be comprised of more than one person, thus supporting the common, scholarly translation of John 1:1? Not only is it possible, but there are living examples in our world today which prove the plausibility and the logical consistency of the Trinity.

Abigail and Brittany Hensel are well known dicepalic twins from New Germany, Minnesota, having two heads, hearts, stomachs and spinal cords, while they share a common bloodstream and all organs below the waist. Abby controls the right limbs, whereas Brittany controls the left, and they share some sensations (but not all) depending on where they originate.[16] Their lives have been publicized since birth in a number of documentaries, the latest of which (at the time if this writing) documents their graduation from Bethel University.

What's interesting about Abby and Brittany, for our consideration, is that they are clearly two distinct persons having two separate centers of consciousness, but they are only one being. They sometimes use the word "I" to refer to themselves individually, but other times to refer to themselves collectively. "I will not be separated," says Brittany. "And I don't have two heads," says Abigail.[17]

While Abby and Brittany are not proof that God is a Trinity, they are proof of the existential plausibility for the concept of the Trinity. In Abby and Brittany there exist multiple persons in a singular being, and because there exists in the natural realm an example of one being comprised of multiple persons, it is conceivable that there may also exist in the supernatural realm a singular being comprised of multiple persons. Of course, God is a spiritual being by nature and not physical, so we shouldn't anthropomorphize our view of God unnecessarily by appealing to the Hensel twins example of physical being. We can only say that it is logically consistent to suggest that God may be one spiritual being comprised of multiple persons if scripture bears that out.

Many JWs think that calling God one and three at the same time violates a basic law of logic, the law of noncontradiction, but this is a simple confusion of the categories of person and being. The law of noncontradiction says that contradictory statements cannot both be true at the same time and in the same sense. For example, when it is said that Abby and Brittany are both one and two there is no contradiction because they are not one and two in the same sense. They are one in the sense of being, and two in the sense of persons. Likewise, when we say that God is both one and three we are not saying that God is one and three in the same sense. God is one in the sense of being, but three in the sense of persons. Thus, there is no inherent logical contradiction in the Trinitarian view.

Another mistake JWs often make when assessing the Trinitarian view is to assume that God's nature must be so construed as to reflect the nature of man. Why, for example, couldn't God's nature be more similar to that of cherubim? Ezekiel describes them as follows:

> Each one had four faces. The first face was the face of a cherub, the second face was the face of a man, the third the face of a lion, and the fourth the face of an eagle [...]. These are the living beings that I saw beneath the God of Israel by the river Chebar; so I knew that they were cherubim. Each one had four faces and each one four wings, and beneath their wings was the form of human hands. (Ezek 10:14,20,21, NASB)

I am not inferring from this passage that the multiple faces of cherubim suggests that they are singular beings comprised of multiple persons (they may or may not be); rather, I'm suggesting that the supernatural realm of creatures described in passages such as this indicates that the constitution of man is not the archetype for the rest of the created order, nor should man be regarded as the template by which we view God.

Nowhere does scripture declare that the One true God, Jehovah, is comprised of only one person, similar to the constitution of man, so what reason do we have to think that His being is so comprised? Perhaps our innate egocentricity misinforms our understanding of God's nature and our imaginations are stunted because of it.

Regardless, having sufficiently dispensed with the notion that the Trinity is an essentially incoherent construct, let's address the JW dispute that says Jesus Christ cannot be one with God in being because Jesus was created, whereas God, by definition, is uncreated and therefore the concept of the Trinity wrongly combines the uncreated God with a "begotten" Jesus of Nazareth. How can a created man be one person of a Trinitarian God who is incorporeal and immortal by nature? Aren't the two mutually exclusive?

God Incognito

First, let's recall what scripture says about Jesus before he became a man:

> In the beginning was the Word, and the Word was with God, and the Word was God. He was with God in the beginning. All things were created through Him, and apart from Him not one thing was created that has been created. (Jn 1:1-3)

> Jesus said unto them, Verily, verily, I say unto you, Before Abraham was born, I am. (Jn 8:58, ASV)

Before the Word became flesh, the Father, the Son (i.e., the pre-incarnate Word), and the Holy Spirit were spirit by nature. As scripture affirms, God in his natural state is spirit. Then the Word became flesh. He left the glory he had with the Father before the world existed (Jn 17:5), humbled himself and took the form of a servant:

> The Word became flesh and took up residence among us. We observed His glory, the glory as the One and Only Son from the Father, full of grace and truth. (Jn 1:14, HCSB)

> But when the fullness of time came, God sent forth His Son, born of a woman, born under the Law. (Gal 4;4, NASB)

> [...] Christ Jesus, who, although He existed in the form of God, did not regard equality with God a thing to be held onto, but emptied Himself, taking the form of a bond-servant, and being made in the likeness of men. Being found in appearance as a man, He humbled

Himself by becoming obedient to the point of death, even death on a cross. (Phil 2:5-8)

When the Word became flesh, he did not cease to be God, nor did he lose any necessary attributes of deity, though he willingly emptied himself of his Godly prerogatives for some time. There was nothing subtracted from his nature by virtue of becoming man; rather, there was an addition to his nature of the essential attributes of man (i.e., a body).

A common JW response to this is that the Bible says, "God is not a man [...]" (Num 23:19), therefore, Jehovah could not become a man or this statement would be falsified. However, this argument ignores the context in which that statement was made. That text, written in the 1400s B.C., does not say that God cannot become a man should He so choose; it merely says that God is not a man that He should lie. It is true that when the book of Numbers was written the Word had not yet become flesh; God had not yet become man. More importantly, that statement was intended to communicate that God's character is unlike fallen man's character in that His doesn't change. It is similar to the statement made by the apostle Paul in his letter to the Romans: "Let God be found true, but every man a liar" (Rom 3:4, ASV). Of course, JW's would agree that Paul wasn't implying that all men, including Jesus, are liars.

When scripture paints in broad strokes we err in taking its meaning too narrowly. We mistakenly promote a sort of balloon animal doctrine when we inflate one verse or passage of scripture beyond its intended meaning and then combine it with other exegetically distended passages, thus supporting a novel theological perspective (*look, a giraffe!*). As the saying goes, context is king. There is an immediate context and a broader context, and both need to be harmonized. Stated another way: when considering the details we must always mind the metanarrative.

Works Cited

[1] A.W. Tozer, *The Knowledge of the Holy* (New York: HarperCollins, 1961).

[2] "Nicene Creed," *Encyclopædia Britannica*. Encyclopædia Britannica Online. Encyclopædia Britannica Inc., 2014. Web. 20 Mar. 2014 http://www.britannica.com/EBchecked/topic/413955/Nicene-Creed.

[3] Glenn Peoples, "God Died," *Right Reason*, Web. 12 July, 2014. http://www.rightreason.org/2013/god-died/

[4] Ibid.

[5] Bauckham, Richard, *Jesus and the God of Israel:* God Crucified *and Other Studies on the New Testament's Divine Identity* (Grand Rapids, Michigan: Wm. B. Eerdmans Publishing Co., 2008), Kindle, section 2.8.

[6] Bauckham, Richard, *Jesus and the God of Israel:* God Crucified *and Other Studies on the New Testament's Divine Identity* (Grand Rapids, Michigan: Wm. B. Eerdmans Publishing Co., 2008), Kindle, section 3.3.2.

[7] Lynn Lundquist, *The Tetragrammaton and the Christian Greek Scriptures* (Word Resources, Inc.; 2nd Edition, 1998).

[8] Bauckham, Richard, *Jesus and the God of Israel:* God Crucified *and Other Studies on the New Testament's Divine Identity* (Grand Rapids, Michigan: Wm. B. Eerdmans Publishing Co., 2008), Kindle, section 7.8. (emphasis mine).

[9] Bauckham, Richard, *Jesus and the God of Israel:* God Crucified *and Other Studies on the New Testament's Divine Identity* (Grand Rapids, Michigan: Wm. B. Eerdmans Publishing Co., 2008), Kindle, section 7.2.

[10] C.S. Lewis, "What Are We to Make of Jesus Christ?" (originally published 1950; this edition from *The Essential C.S. Lewis* [Touchstone, 1996]) 330.

[11] Bauckham, Richard, *Jesus and the God of Israel: God Crucified and Other Studies on the New Testament's Divine Identity* (Grand Rapids, Michigan: Wm. B. Eerdmans Publishing Co., 2008), Kindle, section 2.7.

[12] Ravi Zacharias, *The Uniqueness of Christ in History*, Web 14 Oct., 2014, http://www.rzim.org/let-my-people-think-broadcasts/the-uniqueness-of-christ-in-history-part-1-of-2/

[13] John Stott, "Is Jesus Christ Truth for the 21st Century?" Veritas Forum, Harvard University, 1 Jan. 1994, transcribed http://veritas.org/talks/jesus-christ-truth-21st-century1/

[14] This question was rhetorical and was meant to elicit a thoughtful answer from the rich young ruler so as to provide insight into Jesus's identity, very much similar to the question Jesus asked the disciples in Mark 16:13-17.

[15] Watch Tower Bible and Tract Society of Pennsylvania, 2005, September 2013 Printing, *What Does the Bible Really Teach?* [Data file]. Retrieved from http://www.jw.org/download/?output=html&pub=bh&fileformat=PDF&allangs=0&langwritten=E&txtCMSLang=E&isBible=0

[16] Robert Hommel, "Conjoined Twins and the Trinity: Can One Person be with Another and yet Be the Same Being?" Web. 19 Mar. 2014. http://www.forananswer.org/Top_JW/TwinsTrinity.htm

[17] Ibid.

www.ingramcontent.com/pod-product-compliance
Lightning Source LLC
Chambersburg PA
CBHW031429290426
44110CB00011B/593